THE UNIVERSAL U
DISCOVERING THE "U" IN UNIVERSE

The Universal U: Discovering the "U" in Universe

ISBN 979-8-218-11844-0

Illustrated by Crystal Jefferson

NougyeMukoma.com

THE UNIVERSAL U

DISCOVERING THE "U" IN UNIVERSE

By Nougye Mutungi Mukoma

Illustrated by Crystal Jefferson

"May I forever be the mind & body through which the all mighty creator fulfills its will. I am Grateful!"

Nougye Mutungi Mukoma

TO MY PILLARS

the people who support me

This book is for Miyah, Anastasia, Emmie, Ella, & Justin and of course Saayah, Socce, Simon, Jeffrey, Soleil, Skylar, Alliana, Ethan, Gabrielle, Gianna, Gio, Nathan, Elt-Anne, Renold, Journee and all other amazing little girls and boys! Know you are special and the most amazing stars of this cosmic Universe!

To my most beautiful family, you are my mirrors, my strength, and my compass! My husband, the Universe is grand, you are a special being! My children, the learning of my life, you balance me, and help me to reach for greater truths. May you find your true path.

To the most supportive environment of friends, family, and insightful encounters, I hope this book reveals the significance of the inner truth for you however you perceive this world! My meaningful circle, thank you!

"God goes by many names and can be approached in many forms. Whatever name you choose to call him is how he will show up for you."

Melekh King • **Bon Dieu** Good God

Netjer God • **Yireh** Provider

El Roi Strength • **Melekh** King

EL Elyon Most High God

Creator • **Ngai** Creator

Adonai Lord of Lords

Elohim Creator

El Shaddai Almighty

Yahweh I AM

Olam Eternal God

Tsuri My Rock • Olam Eternal God

HEY "U"!

hi!

hola!

alo!

You are wonderful and unique! There will never be another human like you. No one else can tell your story or see the world the way you do.

hai!

salut!

hallo!

こんにちは

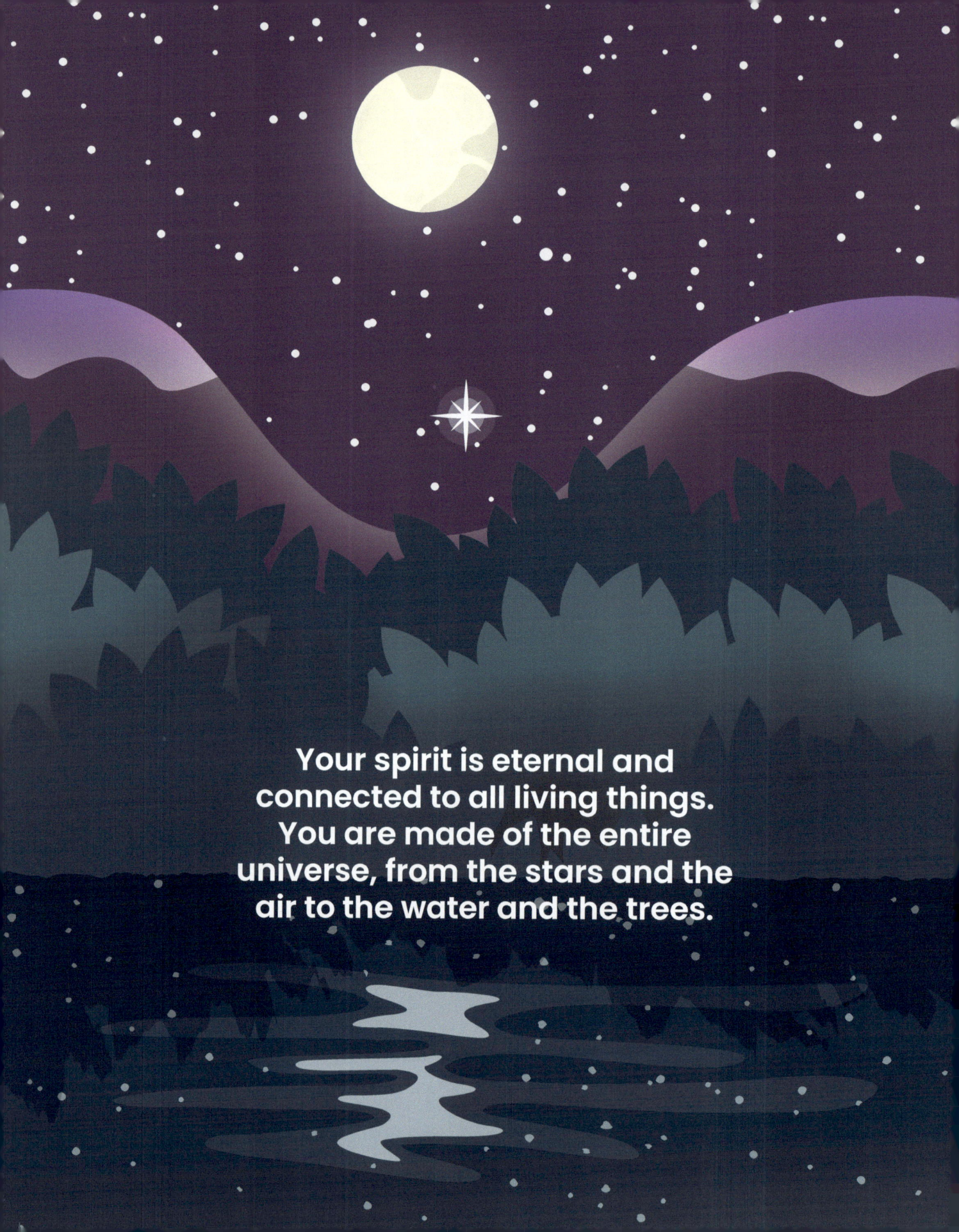

Your spirit is eternal and connected to all living things. You are made of the entire universe, from the stars and the air to the water and the trees.

Just as a seed is planted in Mother Earth, you were planted inside your earthly mother. You are a perfect miracle of nature!

When you took your first breath, your new life began. You entered this world through your mother's womb, and gained a body that your spirit lives in.

Your body stretched and grew just right to get ready for the great things you came here to be and the wondeful things you came here to do.

Your body is one-of-a-kind and is connected to all the generations of ancestors who came before you.

Your grandparents and their parents will always be a part of your physical body and your spiritual body, too.

You were beautifully made.
This is the truth!

You were given the power in your heart to create what you see in your mind. Just as the sun's power makes the flowers grow, the power in your heart makes your vision come to life.

follow your heart

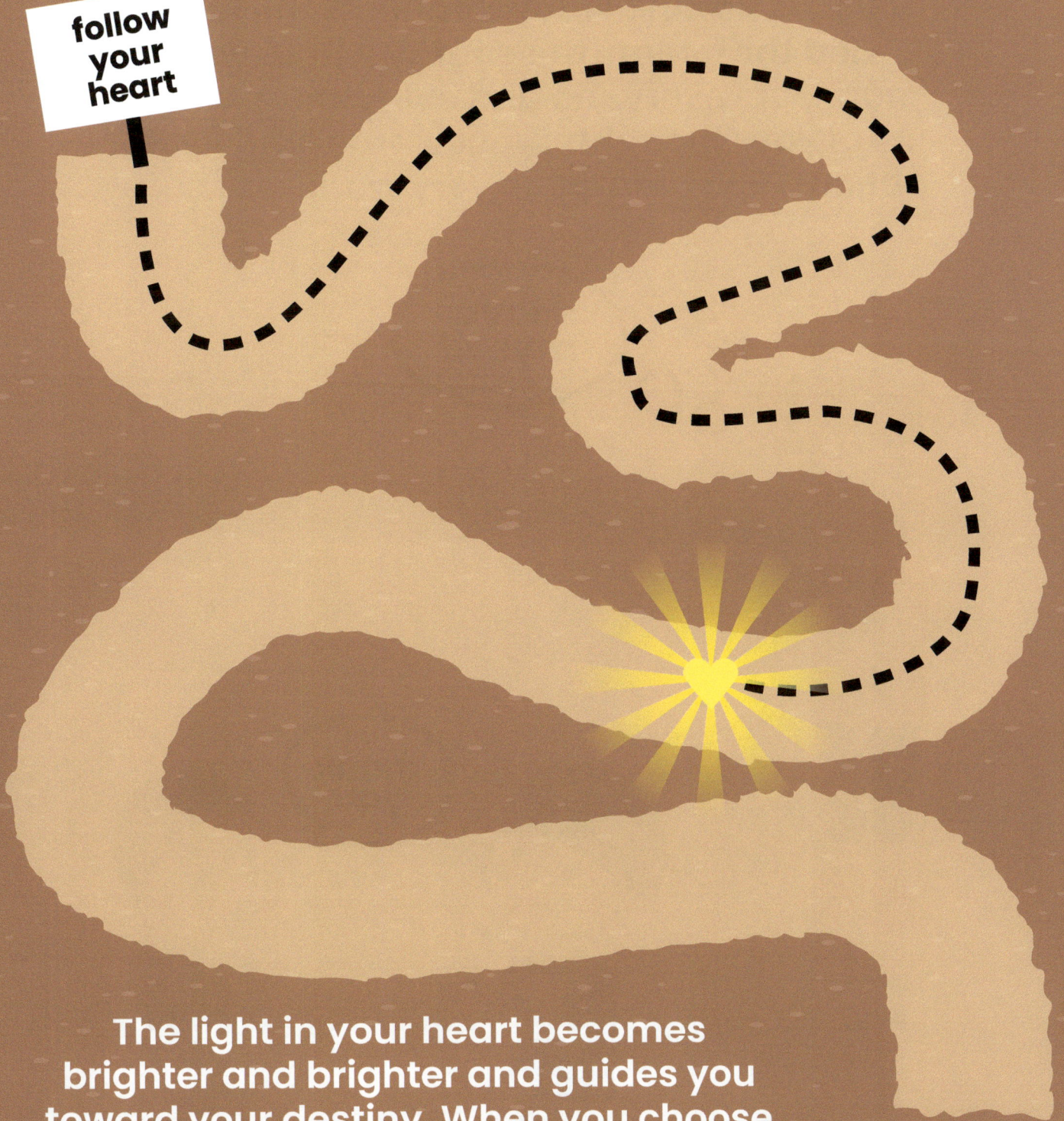

YOUR DESTINY

The light in your heart becomes brighter and brighter and guides you toward your destiny. When you choose happiness, love, and compassion, you choose your true self and unity.

Just as flowing water connects the land and the ocean, the energy within you connects everyone and everything. With all of your thoughts, your words, and your actions, you create the very world you see.

save our planet!

You help your spirit grow strong and reach its full potential when you shine brightly.

You can be whoever you want to be, go wherever you want to go, and achieve anything you want to achieve.

All you have to do is believe!

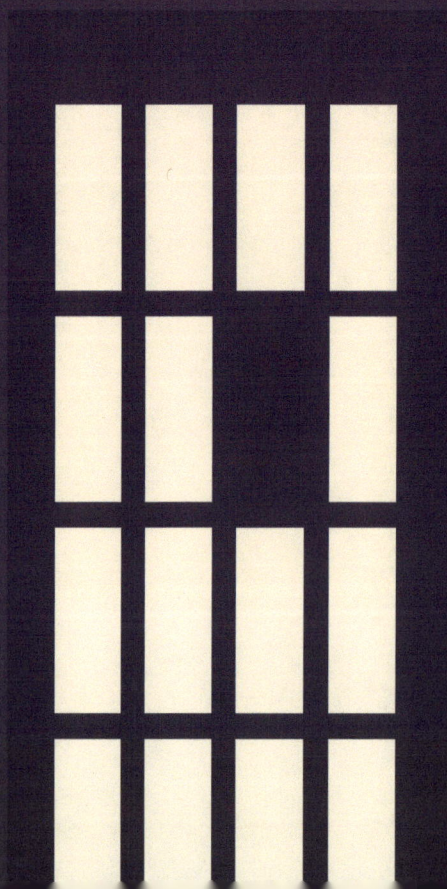

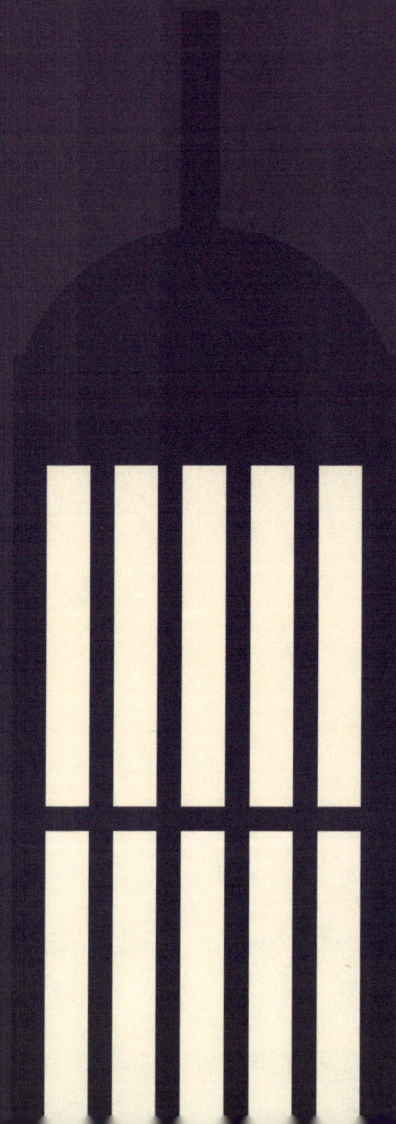

With your energy, you can change your world for the better. Positive energy creates a world full of peace, harmony, and the best vibes ever.

Find out what you love to do and share the joy it brings with old friends and new. Choose to live a positive life and the Universe will reward you.

With great friends, good
fun, and unconditional love,
it is easy to see exactly
what you are made of.

You have so much to offer humanity.
You have the world in your hands!

"U" are a part of the Universe,
so you are destined for greatness!

Let your light shine bright!

"God goes by many names and can be approached in many forms. Whatever name you choose to call him is how he will show up for you."

Elohim Creator • El Shaddai Almighty • Adonai Lord of Lords • Yahweh I AM • Ngai Creator • El Elyon Most High God • Netjer God • Yireh Provider • Olam Eternal God • Tsuri My Rock • El Roi Strength • Melekh King • Bon Dieu Good God

Haiti

HI, I'M NOUGYE!

Nougye Mutungi Mukoma was created with love by the most amazing beings—Marie and Jean Joseph—in the most beautiful country, Haiti. The United States became her home country where she has been a nurse and nurse practitioner for over 12 years.

Nougye believes in the holistic and spiritual aspect of this world, and her life as a wife and mother has aided her spiritual journey in many ways. She lives by universal laws and values on a daily basis in her home life, her work life, and most importantly her spiritual life.

www.ingramcontent.com/pod-product-compliance
Lightning Source LLC
Chambersburg PA
CBHW061147030426
42335CB00002B/132

* 9 7 9 8 2 1 8 1 1 8 4 4 0 *